UNLOCKING YOUR POTENTIAL

Empowering Women through Purpose and Vision

BY

OLUWATOSIN OLAJUMOKE ARODUDU

Books may be purchased by contacting the Author and Publisher at:

info@hadarcreations.com
ooainspires@gmail.com
Cover Design: Hadar Creations
Edited by: Hadar Creations
Interior Design: Hadar Creations
Publisher: Hadar Creations
ISBN: 979-8-89145-664-8

TABLE OF CONTENTS

DEDICATION...6

ACKNOWLEDGEMENT 8

WHY IS THIS BOOK BENEFICIAL TO YOU?.....................9

PART ONE **13**

UNDERSTANDING PURPOSE 14

UNDERSTANDING VISION 16

THE DIFFERENCE BETWEEN PURPOSE AND VISION.................. 18

HOW TO IDENTIFY YOUR PURPOSE: 21

PART TWO **24**

UNDERSTANDING CLARITY 25

THE IMPORTANCE OF CLARITY IN PURPOSEFUL AND VISIONARY LIVING 27

THE SIGNIFICANCE OF BUILDING SKILLS AS A PURPOSEFUL
AND VISIONARY WOMAN 30

PART THREE **34**

HOW TO BIRTH VISION OUT OF PURPOSE............................ 35

HOW TO UNLEASH YOUR TALENTS AND POWER 38

PART FOUR **41**

AUTHENTICITY 42

WISDOM 44

THE RELATIONSHIP BETWEEN AUTHENTICITY AND WISDOM: 45

PART FIVE **49**

OPPOSITION AGAINST VISION 50

HOW TO PROTECT YOURSELF FROM DESTRUCTIVE CRITICISM
AGAINST YOUR VISION 53

NEHEMIAH: A CASE STUDY IN HANDLING OPPOSITION AGAINST VISION
(NEHEMIAH 4) 56

EIGHT VITAL STEPS YOU NEED TO TAKE IN PURSUING YOUR OWN VISION 61

PART SIX **64**

THE POWER OF PASSION FOR A PURPOSEFUL WOMAN 65

THE POWER OF FOCUS FOR VISIONARIES 70

HOW TO APPLY THE POWER OF DISCIPLINE TO ACHIEVE FOCUS 72

PART SEVEN **74**

AVOIDING SELF-COMPARISON AS A PURPOSEFUL AND VISIONARY WOMAN 75

HOW A PURPOSEFUL AND VISIONARY WOMAN CAN AVOID SELF COMPARISON 78

PART EIGHT **81**

DEALING WITH UNHEALTHY COMPETITION AS A PURPOSEFUL AND VISIONARY
WOMAN 82

HOW TO AVOID UNHEALTHY COMPETITION AS A PURPOSEFUL AND VISIONARY
WOMAN 85

FINAL NOTE **88**

REFERENCES **90**

ABOUT THE AUTHOR **91**

OTHER BOOKS BY AUTHOR **94**

THE DISCIPLINED WRITER 95

TRAPPED IN TRAUMA 97

UNVEILED 99

NURTURING EXCELLENCE 101

EMPOWERED LEADERSHIP 103

THE VISIONARY LIFE 105

IDENTITY 107

JOURNAL **110**

DEDICATION

With utmost humility, I offer this book as a dedicated tribute to the almighty God, the divine wellspring of inspiration and wisdom. It is by His divine calling that I have embarked upon this transformative undertaking, and I humbly acknowledge and attribute all honor and glory to Him.

To the Woman Who Will Read This Book,

This dedication is a heartfelt tribute to you and the incredible journey you are about to start. As you hold this book in your hands, I want you to know that it is crafted with deep love, an unwavering belief in your potential, and the utmost respect for the unique path you are taking.

You are a woman of strength, resilience, and boundless potential. You possess within you a spark of greatness waiting to be ignited. It is my sincere hope that as you delve into the pages of this book, you will discover the transformative power of purpose and vision in your life.

May these words resonate with the depths of your being, awakening a sense of clarity, direction, and empowerment within you. May they guide you toward a profound understanding of your purpose, allowing you to navigate life's twists and turns with unwavering focus and determined belief in your ability to live a life that aligns with your deepest desires.

This book is not just a collection of ideas and theories; it is a roadmap tailored to your unique journey. It is a companion that will travel with you, offering guidance, inspiration, and practical tools to help you unlock your full potential. Through thought-provoking exercises, insightful reflections, and empowering practices, it will equip you to embrace your true worth, live with intention, and make a meaningful impact in the world.

As you turn each page, may you be reminded of your innate strength, your limitless potential, and the incredible value you bring to the world. May you embrace the challenges and setbacks as opportunities for growth and transformation, and may you celebrate every milestone and success along the way.

Remember, dear reader, that you are not alone on this journey. You are part of a community of remarkable women who are also striving to discover their purpose and unleash their visions. Together, we stand united, cheering each other on, and celebrating the brilliance that lies within each one of us.

I dedicate this book to you, the woman who dares to dream, who has the courage to chase her visions, and who is committed to living a life of purpose and impact. May it serve as a guiding light, illuminating your path and reminding you of the extraordinary power that resides within you.

With heartfelt gratitude and admiration,
Oluwatosin Olajumoke Arodudu

ACKNOWLEDGEMENT

I extend my heartfelt gratitude to the Almighty God, the source of inspiration and vision. It is through His divine grace that I received a vision, even when I felt unqualified to embrace and nurture it. All glory and praise belong to Him, for His guidance and empowerment throughout this remarkable journey. With His grace, I have walked this path with faith, strength, and purpose.

To my beloved husband, the one who believes in me, my unwavering support throughout my journey of discovery and purposeful living up to this point, I express my deepest appreciation. You have been my constant source of encouragement, never hindering my growth but always lifting me higher to soar. Your love and unwavering belief in me have been my guiding light, and for that, I am eternally grateful. May the Lord continue to lead and bless your path abundantly, and may you always shine brightly in all that you do. I love you dearly, my darling husband.

WHY IS THIS BOOK BENEFICIAL TO YOU?

Dear Woman,

I am thrilled to introduce you to my workbook on the power of purpose and vision, designed specifically with you in mind. This workbook holds tremendous value for you to:

1. **Unleash Your Potential**: The workbook serves as a transformative tool to help you tap into your true potential. As you explore the depths of your purpose and vision, you will uncover hidden talents, passions, and strengths that have the power to shape your life in extraordinary ways. It will empower you to break free from limitations and embrace the boundless possibilities that lie within you.

2. **Clarity and Direction**: Are you seeking clarity and direction in your life? This workbook provides a structured and insightful approach to help you gain a clear understanding of your purpose and vision. It offers you thought-provoking exercises and prompts that will enable you to uncover your authentic desires, define your values, and chart a course toward a life filled with meaning and fulfillment.

3. **Overcome Challenges**: Life is full of challenges and obstacles that can sometimes make us question our path. The workbook equips you with tools and strategies to navigate these hurdles with resilience and grace. It will empower you to stay focused on your purpose, overcome setbacks, and use adversity as fuel for growth. With this resource as your companion, you will build the inner strength and determination you need to overcome any obstacle that shows up in your way.

4. **Boost Confidence and Self-Belief:** Developing a deep sense of confidence and self-belief is essential for success and fulfillment. Through the workbook's exercises and reflective practices, you will gain a profound understanding of your

unique qualities, talents, and worth. It will encourage you to embrace your strengths, recognize your achievements, and cultivate an unshakable belief in your ability to create the life you envision.

5. **Live with Intention**: The workbook will empower you to live life with intention and purpose. It will guide you in setting meaningful goals that are aligned with your vision, helping you prioritize your time, energy, and resources. By embracing intentional living, you will experience a sense of fulfillment and satisfaction as you make deliberate choices that propel you toward your vision and create a life of purposeful impact.

6. **Connect with a Supportive Community**: As you embark on this journey of discovering and embracing your purpose and vision, you will join a community of like-minded women who are also on their own paths to transformation. This supportive network offers encouragement, inspiration, and a safe space to share experiences and insights. Together, we can uplift and empower one another as we navigate the beautiful complexities of life.

I invite you to embark on this empowering journey with me. Let us delve into the pages of the workbook and unlock the incredible power of purpose and vision within you. It is time to embrace your unique gifts, shape your destiny, and create a life that ignites your soul!

With warmest regards,
#OOA

PART ONE

UNDERSTANDING PURPOSE

Purpose is the reason for which something is done or created, or the goal or objective to be achieved. It can also refer to a sense of meaning or direction in one's life, often related to a person's values, passions, and aspirations. In some cases, people may have a specific, clear purpose they are working toward, while in other cases, they may be searching for a sense of purpose or meaning in their lives. Purpose gives a new meaning to life. It makes it interesting because there is something exciting that one looks forward to every day.

For a woman who has healed from her trauma, and is on her self-discovery journey, purpose is a deeply personal and empowering process. It involves discovering and embracing the unique passions, talents, and values that resonate within your heart. Purpose, in this context, can be seen as the alignment between one's authentic self and the impact they desire to make in the world.

It means recognizing your innate gifts and strengths, and understanding how you can use these qualities to contribute positively to your life and the lives of others. It involves identifying the activities, causes, or roles that bring you fulfillment, joy, and a sense of meaning.

For a woman on her self-discovery journey, purpose may manifest in various forms, such as pursuing a career or vocation that aligns with your values, committing yourself to a cause you are passionate about, nurturing and uplifting your family, or even being influential within your community. It is about living a life that is driven by your inner calling and making a meaningful impact in your spheres of influence.

Purpose for the women on this kind of journey goes beyond external achievements and societal expectations. It is about living in alignment with their authentic selves, embracing their unique journey, and making choices that honor their values and passions. It is a continuous exploration and evolution, as they navigate their self-discovery journey and unleash their fullest potential.

This has been my story, and this is why I have put together my journey of self-discovery in a course series comprising five books, with this being the third, in order to liberate women. The best way to be a blessing to lives is by documenting your journey to light the way for others who are coming behind you.

UNDERSTANDING VISION

A vision is a mental image or concept of a desired future state or outcome. It can be a long-term goal or a broad, overarching idea of what one wants to achieve.

In a business setting, a vision statement is a statement that describes the company's aspirations for the future and what it hopes to achieve. In an individual context, a vision is one's personal aspiration and the life one hopes to create for oneself.

It is an idea or image of something to be created, an intended direction, or a desired outcome. It is a long-term goal that inspires and guides an organization or an individual toward a future reality. Simply put, a vision is a future you want to create out of your purpose, the future you see in your pursuit of purpose.

For you, a woman who is on a self-discovery journey, defining vision involves tapping into your inner desires, aspirations, and dreams to create a clear and compelling picture of the future you visualize for herself. Vision, in this context, is a guiding force that provides direction, purpose, and inspiration as she moves forward in her j self-discovery journey.

Defining vision begins with introspection and reflection. It involves exploring your passions, values, strengths, and interests to gain a deep understanding of what truly matters to you. By connecting with your authentic self, you can uncover the unique contributions you want to make and the impact you desire to have personally and on others.

As a woman on a self-discovery journey, you may define your vision by picturing the kind of life you want to lead, the experiences you want to have, the goals you want to achieve, and the values you want to embody. It goes beyond short-term objectives and encompasses a broader perspective of your desired future, taking into account various aspects such as relationships, career, personal growth, health, and overall well-being.

Vision for a woman on a self-discovery journey is not set in stone. It is a dynamic and evolving process that you adjust as you continue to learn, grow, and explore new dimensions of yourself. It serves as a compass, guiding your choices and actions, and inspiring you to step out of your comfort zone, embrace challenges, and pursue opportunities aligned with your authentic desires.

By defining your vision as a woman on a self-discovery journey, you gain clarity, motivation, and a sense of purpose. It becomes a powerful tool that empowers you to make intentional decisions, set meaningful goals, and navigate your path with confidence and resilience. It becomes a source of inspiration and a reminder of the limitless possibilities that await you as you embrace your true self and live a purposeful life.

THE DIFFERENCE BETWEEN PURPOSE AND VISION

Purpose and vision are closely related concepts, but they have distinct meanings and serve different purposes in a person's life.

Purpose

Purpose refers to the underlying reason or motivation behind one's actions, existence, or pursuits. It is the deep sense of meaning, significance, and direction that drives an individual. Purpose answers the fundamental question of "why" - why someone does what they do, why they strive for certain goals, and why they make particular choices.

Three key characteristics of purpose include:

1. **Inner Calling**: Purpose arises from within, often rooted in a person's passions, values, and core beliefs. It reflects their authentic selves and what truly matters to them.

2. **Long-Term Perspective**: Purpose extends beyond short-term goals. It encompasses a broader, enduring sense of meaning and fulfillment. It provides a sense of direction and guides a person's overall life trajectory.

3. **Universal Impact:** Purpose typically involves making a positive difference, contributing to something larger than oneself, and serving others or a greater cause. It has a societal or collective dimension.

Vision

Vision, on the other hand, is a future-oriented concept that represents a desired outcome or a mental picture of what someone wants to achieve or create. It is a clear, inspiring, and specific representation of what one envisions for themselves or their endeavors. Vision answers the question of "what" - what someone aspires to become, what they want to accomplish, or what they want their life or work to look like.

Three key characteristics of vision include:

1. **Clarity and Specificity:** Vision is well-defined and articulated with precision. It captures the desired state or outcome in a vivid and detailed manner.

2. **Inspirational and Motivating**: Vision ignites enthusiasm, passion, and motivation. It serves as a source of inspiration and energizes individuals to pursue their goals and overcome challenges.

3. **Flexibility and Adaptability**: Vision can be adjusted or refined over time as circumstances change or new opportunities arise. It remains aligned with one's purpose but allows for flexibility on the way and even in strategies adopted to achieve the desired outcome.

In summary, purpose is the underlying driving force and meaning behind one's actions, while vision represents the specific desired outcome or future state one envisions.

Purpose provides the "why" and guides one's overall life direction, while vision provides the "what" and inspires focused action toward a specific goal or desired future.

Both purpose and vision are important in shaping a person's journey of self-discovery, personal growth, and fulfillment.

HOW TO IDENTIFY YOUR PURPOSE:

Embarking on a self-discovery journey is a powerful step toward understanding oneself deeply and uncovering personal purpose. Here are seven steps you can take as a woman to identify your purpose:

1. **Reflect on Passions and Interests**: Start by exploring activities, subjects, or causes that ignite joy and genuine enthusiasm in you. Reflect on what brings you fulfillment and satisfaction, both in personal life and career aspirations.

2. **Assess Strengths and Talents**: Recognize and embrace your distinctive strengths and natural talents. Consider the unique skills that you effortlessly exhibit, and which bring you a sense of accomplishment. Identifying these can provide clues to areas where you can excel and make meaningful impact.

3. **Identify Core Values:** Reflect on the values that are most important to and resonant with you. Your core values shape your beliefs, guide decision-making, and define what truly matters to you. Aligning personal purpose with these values can evoke a deep sense of meaning and fulfillment in you.

4. **Seek Inspiration and Role Models**: Look for individuals who have found their purpose and are living authentic, fulfilling lives. Learn from their experiences, read their stories, and find inspiration in their strategies to align their passions with their purpose.

5. **Explore New Experiences**: Step outside of your comfort zone and try new things. Engage in activities or projects that spark curiosity and provide opportunities for growth and self-discovery. New experiences often lead to unexpected insights and can help you unearth your hidden passions.

6. **Practice Self-Reflection and Journaling**: Dedicate regular time to introspection and self-reflection. Journaling can be a powerful tool to explore your thoughts, emotions, and desires. Write freely without judgment and allow your thoughts to flow unhindered. This gives room for patterns to emerge.

7. **Seek Support and Guidance**: Connect with mentors, coaches, or like-minded individuals who can provide you with support and guidance throughout the self-discovery journey. Engage in meaningful conversations and garner external perspectives to obtain valuable insights and receive encouragement.

Remember, the process of discovering one's purpose is personal and unique. It may take time and experimentation, and it may evolve over time. Embrace the journey with openness, patience, and self-compassion, allowing the purpose to unfold naturally. Practice self-compassion as sometimes you might make mistakes. Also, allow yourself to learn from your mistakes and evolve. Do not stagnate or self-destruct in the process, rather grow and transform into a higher version of yourself.

PART TWO

UNDERSTANDING CLARITY

Clarity, in relation to purpose, refers to a deep understanding and a clear vision of one's true calling or reason for being. It involves a keen sense of focus, direction, and conviction about the path one should pursue in life. Clarity of purpose provides a clear sense of identity, meaning, and direction, guiding choices and actions in alignment with one's values and passions.

When you have clarity of purpose, you possess a strong sense of self-awareness, knowing who you are and what you want to achieve. You have an explicit understanding of your unique strengths, values, and interests, which helps you make decisions and set goals that are in harmony with your purpose.

Clarity of purpose brings a sense of inner knowing and confidence, enabling you to navigate challenges, setbacks, and distractions with resilience and determination. It acts as a compass, guiding actions and choices toward a fulfilling and meaningful life.

Having clarity of purpose also involves being able to articulate and communicate your purpose effectively to yourself and others. It is the ability to express the essence of your purpose in a concise and compelling manner, guiding others to understand and connect with it.

In summary, clarity in relation to purpose entails having a clear understanding of your unique calling, values, and aspirations, which guides decision-making, actions, and communication toward alignment with that purpose. It stimulates a sense of focus, direction, and fulfillment in your life journey.

- 26 -

THE IMPORTANCE OF CLARITY IN PURPOSEFUL AND VISIONARY LIVING

Clarity plays a crucial role for a woman in living a purposeful and visionary life.

It helps you to articulate and align your purpose and vision. It keeps you focused and grounded.

Six key reasons why clarity is vital to living a purposeful and visionary life are:

1. **Alignment with Authentic Self:** Clarity allows you as a woman to connect with your authentic self as you understand your true desires, values, and passions. It helps you live a life that is true to yourself and avoid the trap of conforming to societal expectations or pursuing goals that do not align with your core essence. When you have clarity, you can make choices and take actions that reflect who you genuinely are.

2. **Guiding Life Decisions**: Clarity provides a clear framework for making important life decisions. It helps you discern which opportunities and paths are in alignment with your purpose and vision. With clarity, you can navigate through choices with confidence, knowing that your decisions are taking you closer to your desired outcomes.

3. **Meaningful Goal Setting**: Clarity empowers you to set significant and inspiring goals. When you have a clear understanding of your purpose and vision, you can set goals that are in tandem with your larger life direction. This ensures that your goals are not just driven by external pressures or societal norms but are rooted in your personal values and aspirations. This gives you a sense of fulfillment and purpose as you work toward them.

4. **Focus and Prioritization**: Clarity helps you focus your energy, time, and resources on what truly matters. By knowing your purpose and vision, she can prioritize activities and commitments that contribute to your overall goals. This enables you to avoid distractions, say no to things that do not align with your vision, and create space for what is tremendously important in your life.

5. **Resilience and Motivation**: Clarity provides a strong sense of direction and meaning, acting as a source of motivation and resilience. When faced with challenges or setbacks as woman with clarity, choose to stay focused on your purpose, draw upon your intrinsic motivation, and find the strength to persevere. Clarity serves as a guiding light during difficult times, helping you stay committed to your vision.

6. **Inspiring Others**: A woman who lives with clarity and purpose becomes an inspiration to others. Your clarity radiates authenticity, passion, and determination, which inspire those around you to also seek and live purpose-driven lives. By

embodying your vision, you unleash the potential to positively impact and influence others.

In summary, clarity is essential for you in living a purposeful and visionary life as it aligns you with your authentic self, guides your decision-making, helps you set meaningful goals, fosters focus and resilience, and brings inspiration to others. It allows you to lead a deeply fulfilling, impactful life which is in harmony with your true calling.

THE SIGNIFICANCE OF BUILDING SKILLS AS A PURPOSEFUL AND VISIONARY WOMAN

Building skills refers to the process of acquiring and developing abilities, knowledge, and competencies in a specific area. Building skills is of paramount importance for a purposeful and visionary woman. Below are eight reasons why skill development is crucial for a purposeful and visionary woman:

1. **Empowerment**: Developing skills empowers you to take control of your own destiny and pursue your purpose with confidence. It equips you with the tools and knowledge needed to overcome challenges, make informed decisions, and navigate your chosen path.

2. **Amplifying Potential:** Skill development unlocks your full potential, allowing you to excel in your chosen endeavors. By acquiring new skills and honing existing ones, you expand your capabilities and become more effective in pursuing your vision. This amplification of potential propels you closer to achieving your goals.

3. **Adaptability**: In a rapidly changing world, building skills ensures that you remain adaptable and resilient. Acquiring new competencies equips you with the flexibility to respond to evolving circumstances, seize new opportunities, and navigate through unexpected challenges.

4. **Enhancing Confidence**: Skill development boosts your self-confidence and self-assurance. As you gain proficiency in various areas, you develop a sense of mastery and belief in your abilities. This confidence empowers you to take on ambitious goals, overcome self-doubt, and persevere in the face of obstacles.

5. **Expanding Influence:** Building skills expands your sphere of influence and opens doors to new opportunities. With enhanced expertise, you can make a more significant impact in your chosen field or industry. This increased influence

allows you to inspire and mentor others, creating a positive ripple effect within your community and beyond.

6. **Fostering Innovation**: Skills act as catalysts for innovation and creativity. As you build your skills, you become better equipped to generate fresh ideas, think critically, and solve complex problems. This ability to innovate fuels your visionary pursuits and propels you toward groundbreaking achievements.

7. **Networking and Collaboration**: Developing skills provides opportunities to connect and collaborate with like-minded individuals. Engaging in skill-building activities, workshops, and training programs allows you to expand your network, forge valuable relationships, and leverage collective knowledge and resources to fuel your purpose and vision.

8. **Continuous Growth and Learning**: Skill development fosters a lifelong commitment to growth and learning. A purposeful and visionary woman understands that growth is an ongoing process. By continuously building new skills, you ensure your personal and professional development remains aligned with your evolving aspirations.

In my personal journey, starting out as a writer on my blog, oluwatosinarodudu.com, proved to be a transformative experience.

It allowed me to develop numerous skills that bolstered my confidence. I had to learn how to create my own website, produce graphic design for simple visuals, create book covers, and even master the art of designing presentation slides.

In 2018, God planted the idea of becoming a publisher in my heart, and I eagerly embraced the opportunity, further expanding my skill set. These newfound abilities played a pivotal role in boosting my self-confidence after years of unemployment. In fact, they proved instrumental in securing my first formal job as a human resources officer in 2019. During the interview process, I had to deliver a compelling presentation, and my interviewers were incredibly impressed. They repeatedly commended my brilliance. Consequently, I was offered the position.

To delve deeper into this story and explore many more of my personal narratives, I invite you to visit oluwatosinarodudu.com. Additionally, you can partake in my course titled "The Power of Purpose and Vision," which offers valuable insights and guidance. I consider it a privilege to share my knowledge and experiences with you through this course.

In summary, building skills is an integral essence of your journey as a purposeful and visionary woman. It empowers you, amplifies your potential, enhances your confidence, fosters adaptability, expands your influence, fuels innovation, fosters networking and collaboration, and encourages continuous growth and learning.

By investing in skill development, you equip yourself to make a lasting impact and fulfill your purpose with excellence.

PART THREE

HOW TO BIRTH VISION OUT OF PURPOSE

You can birth vision out of purpose by following these nine steps:

1. **Discover your Purpose**: The first step is to gain clarity on your purpose in life. This involves self-reflection, introspection, and understanding your unique strengths, passions, and values. It is important for you as a woman to identify what truly drives and fulfills you.

2. **Set Clear Goals**: Once your purpose is defined, you can set clear and specific goals aligned with it. These goals should be challenging yet attainable, and they should reflect your vision for the future.

3. **Create a Vision**: With a strong sense of purpose and well-defined goals, you can create a compelling vision for yourself as a woman. This vision represents your desired future state, encompassing both personal and professional aspects of your life. It should be inspiring, motivating, and aligned with your purpose.

4. **Develop an Action Plan**: To birth vision out of purpose, you need a well-structured action plan. This plan outlines the specific steps you need to take to bring your vision to life. It includes short-term and long-term strategies, milestones, and timelines.

5. **Cultivate Self-Belief and Confidence:** Believing in yourself and having confidence in your abilities are crucial factors in birthing vision. You must cultivate a positive mindset, overcome self-doubt, and surround yourself with a supportive network that encourages and uplifts you.

6. **Embrace Resilience and Perseverance**: The journey of birthing your vision can be challenging and filled with obstacles. It is important for you to develop resilience and perseverance. You should be prepared to overcome setbacks, learn from failures, and stay committed to your purpose and vision.

7. **Seek Support and Collaboration:** Building a strong support system is essential. You can seek mentors, coaches, or like-minded individuals who can provide guidance, encouragement, and valuable insights. Collaboration with others who share similar visions can also amplify your efforts and bring fresh perspectives.

8. **Take Action and Adjust as Needed:** Birthing vision requires taking consistent action. You should start implementing your action plan, continuously evaluating, and adjusting your strategies as needed. Flexibility and adaptability are crucial in navigating the journey.

9. **Celebrate Milestones and Progress**: Along the way, it is important for you to celebrate your milestones and acknowledge your progress. Recognizing achievements boosts motivation and reinforces your belief in the vision you are birthing.

By following these steps, you can effectively birth vision out of purpose and empower yourself to create a meaningful and fulfilling life aligned with your true calling.

HOW TO UNLEASH YOUR TALENTS AND POWER

1. **Embrace Your Authenticity**: Emphasize your unique qualities and embrace what sets you apart. Recognize that your individuality is a source of strength and power. Be true to yourself and let your authentic self emerge.

2. **Find Your Passion**: Discover what truly ignites your passion and fuels your energy. Explore different interests and activities to uncover what brings you joy and fulfillment. When

you align your talents with your passions, you unleash a powerful force within you.

3. **Take Bold Action**: Step out of your comfort zone and take bold actions to pursue your dreams. Embrace calculated risks and do not let fear hold you back. Trust in your abilities and seize opportunities.

4. **Cultivate a Growth Mindset**: Embrace a mindset of continuous growth and learning. See challenges as opportunities for development and improvement. Acknowledge failure as learning experiences and utilize them to propel you forward. With a growth mindset, you will unlock your full potential.

5. **Build a Supportive Network:** Surround yourself with supportive individuals who believe in you and uplift your spirits. Seek out mentors, role models, and peers who inspire and motivate you. Collaborate with like-minded individuals to amplify your impact and expand your opportunities.

6. **Practice Self-Care:** Prioritize self-care to nurture your physical, mental, and emotional well-being. Take time to rest, recharge, and engage in activities that bring you joy and help you relax. When you prioritize self-care, you empower yourself to show up as your best self.

7. **Develop Effective Communication Skills**: Enhance your communication skills to effectively convey your ideas, needs, and aspirations. Learn to articulate your thoughts with

confidence and assertiveness. Effective communication enables you to influence and inspire others naturally.

8. **Seek and Embrace Feedback**: Welcome feedback from trusted sources to grow and improve. Actively seek constructive criticism and use it as a catalyst for personal and professional development. Healthy feedback helps you refine your talents and enhance your skills.

9. **Celebrate Your Achievements**: Acknowledge and celebrate your accomplishments, no matter how small. Take time to reflect on your progress and the milestones you have achieved. Celebrating your successes boosts your confidence and reinforces your belief in your talent and competence.

10. **Pay it Forward**: Empower and uplift other women around you. Share your knowledge, experiences, and support with others who may benefit from your guidance. By lifting others up, you contribute to a collective empowerment that creates a positive ripple effect.

Remember, each woman has her own unique journey. Embrace your individuality and embrace the power within you. Trust in your abilities, believe in yourself, and pursue your passions with determination and resilience. With God by your side, you will soar and prosper on all sides irrespective of the challenges you might face.

PART FOUR

AUTHENTICITY

Authenticity encompasses staying true to oneself and being genuine. It involves embracing one's values, beliefs, and unique personality instead of conforming to societal norms or living as someone else's copy.

Authentic individuals possess a strong sense of self-awareness and self-acceptance, enabling them to feel comfortable in their own skin. They engage in honest and transparent interactions, consistently remaining true to themselves in various situations.

Maintaining authenticity can be challenging, particularly in a society that often pressures people to conform to specific standards. Nevertheless, authenticity is vital for personal and professional growth. It enables individuals to foster deeper and more meaningful relationships, translating to greater fulfillment and success in their lives.

It is essential to understand that authenticity does not imply perfection. We all have flaws, make mistakes, and have areas to improve upon. Being authentic involves being honest about your strengths and acknowledging your weaknesses.

As a woman, it is common to encounter people who attempt to confine you within gender-bound expectations. However, it is crucial to remain true to yourself and not internalize the negativity they project. By doing so, you will not prove their stereotypes right and you avoid becoming a toxic and negative person.

Instead, focus on staying in your own light, channel your energy toward your purpose and vision, and pursue them with unwavering dedication. This approach has proven effective. You silence the critics, and eventually earn their respect.

WISDOM

Wisdom can be defined as the ability to apply knowledge, experience, understanding, and good judgment to make sound and rational decisions. It involves having a deep insight into the nature of things, recognizing the underlying principles and truths, and using that knowledge to navigate life's challenges and make smart choices.

Wisdom goes beyond intelligence or knowledge. It encompasses a holistic understanding of the complexities of life, including how various factors are interconnected and the consequences of actions. Wisdom involves considering different perspectives, evaluating potential outcomes, and discerning the best course of action based on moral, ethical, and practical considerations.

A wise person possesses clarity of thought, emotional intelligence, and the ability to see beyond immediate circumstances. They draw on their experiences and learnings to make informed decisions, while avoiding impulsive or short-sighted choices. Wisdom also involves humility, to acknowledge that one's knowledge is limited and there is always room for learning and growth.

Wisdom is often associated with age and experience, but it can also be cultivated at any stage of life through reflection, introspection, and a commitment to seeking knowledge and understanding. It is a valuable quality that guides you toward living a fulfilled and purposeful life as you positively influence those around you.

THE RELATIONSHIP BETWEEN AUTHENTICITY AND WISDOM:

Authenticity and wisdom are interconnected and support and strengthen each other. Here is how they correlate:

1. **Self-Awareness**: Both authenticity and wisdom involve a deep level of self-awareness. Authenticity requires knowing and accepting oneself, including one's values, beliefs, strengths, and weaknesses. Wisdom also stems from understanding oneself and recognizing personal biases, limitations, and areas for growth. The more authentic you are, the more you

can tap into your inner wisdom and make choices aligned with your true self.

2. **Emotional Intelligence**: Authenticity and wisdom both involve emotional intelligence. Authentic individuals are in touch with their emotions, express them honestly, and are open to emotional connections with others. Wisdom entails recognizing and understanding emotions, both in yourself and in others, and using that understanding to navigate interpersonal relationships and make empathetic decisions.

3. **Values and Ethics**: Authenticity and wisdom are both rooted in a strong bedrock of values and ethics. Authentic individuals adhere to their values and principles, even in challenging situations. Wisdom guides individuals to make ethical choices based on moral principles and long-term consequences. The alignment of authenticity and wisdom allows you to make decisions that are not only true to themselves but also uphold ethical standards and promote the well-being of others.

4. **Reflective Thinking**: Both authenticity and wisdom involve reflective thinking. Authentic individuals engage in introspection, examining their thoughts, feelings, and actions. Similarly, wisdom necessitates reflecting on experiences, learning from mistakes, and seeking insights that can inform sound future decisions. The practice of self-reflection enhances both authenticity and wisdom, leading to personal growth and a deeper understanding of oneself and the world.

5. **Impact on Others**: Both authenticity and wisdom have a positive impact on those around us. Authentic individuals inspire others by living in alignment with their true selves, encouraging others to do the same. Wise individuals offer guidance, support, and insights based on their accumulated knowledge and experiences. The combination of authenticity and wisdom fosters trust, respect, and meaningful connections with others.

Authenticity and wisdom share a close relationship, often reinforcing one another. When you embrace authenticity, you create an environment conducive to acquiring wisdom by staying true to yourself and remaining open to personal growth and learning. Simultaneously, wisdom supports authenticity by providing you with a deeper understanding of your own identity and your role in the world.

However, it is important to avoid misconstruing authenticity for rudeness or brash behavior, as some women tend to do these days. Such actions can lead you astray from your true self and result in an unpleasant reputation.

It is essential to critically examine your behavior, ensuring that you do not use authenticity as a cover for negative conduct. Authenticity should not be used as a justification for behaving poorly while expecting others to accept it unquestioningly.

Instead, it is crucial to combine authenticity with wisdom. Doing this allows you to pursue your purpose with a positive and enlightened mindset. When you align authenticity and wisdom, you can navigate your path in the light, free from the darkness of negativity.

Overall, authenticity and wisdom are intertwined qualities that boost each other. When you cultivate authenticity, you tap into your inner wisdom, and as you cultivate wisdom, you gain clarity and insight into living authentically. Both qualities positively contribute to personal growth, fulfillment, and the ability to navigate life's challenges with integrity and purpose.

PART FIVE

OPPOSITION AGAINST VISION

When people oppose your vision, it means they hold differing perspectives, opinions, or beliefs that contradict or conflict with your own vision or goals. These individuals may express disagreement, criticism, or resistance toward your ideas, plans, or aspirations.

Opposition to your vision can arise from various reasons, such as:

Differences in values or priorities: People may have contrasting values or priorities that make them perceive your vision differently or focus on alternative objectives.

Fear or uncertainty: Some individuals may resist your vision due to fear of change, uncertainty about its feasibility or outcomes, or concerns about potential risks and challenges involved.

Personal biases or interests: Opposition can stem from personal biases, self-interests, or conflicts of interest that create resistance toward your vision. People may feel threatened or disadvantaged by your proposed direction.

Lack of understanding or communication: Miscommunication or a lack of clarity in conveying your vision can contribute to opposition. If others do not fully grasp your intentions or the potential benefits, they may oppose it based on misconceptions or misunderstandings.

Competition or conflicting agendas: In certain situations, opposing visions may arise due to competitive dynamics, conflicting agendas, or differing objectives within a group or organization.

When you are faced with opposition to your vision, it is important to approach the situation with openness, respect, and a willingness to listen. Seek to understand the concerns and perspectives of those opposing your vision, as it can provide valuable insights and in turn help refine your own ideas. Engage in constructive dialogue, address any misconceptions or fears, and strive to find common ground or potential compromises.

However, it is also important to remain steadfast in your conviction if you genuinely believe in the value and validity of your vision. Evaluate the validity of the opposing views, assess potential risks and benefits, and make informed decisions. It may be necessary to respectfully defend and advocate for your vision, while also being open to adapting or adjusting certain aspects if warranted.

Remember that opposition to your vision can sometimes be an opportunity for growth, learning, and improvement. By addressing concerns, engaging in dialogue, and maintaining confidence in your vision, you can navigate and overcome obstacles, moving closer to achieving your goals.

HOW TO PROTECT YOURSELF FROM DESTRUCTIVE CRITICISM AGAINST YOUR VISION

1. **Stay grounded in self-belief**: Develop a strong sense of self-belief and confidence in your vision. Remind yourself of your strengths, accomplishments, and the value of your ideas. Trust in your abilities and the validity of your vision. These will help shield you from destructive criticism.

2. **Seek support from trusted allies**: Surround yourself with a supportive network of trusted individuals who believe in you and your vision. Seek feedback and guidance from those who have your best interests at heart and can provide constructive input and encouragement.

3. **Choose your audience wisely:** Be selective about whom you share your vision with. Not everyone will appreciate or understand your goals, so focus on sharing your ideas with supportive, open-minded individuals who align with your vision. Seek out mentors, advisors, or like-minded individuals who can provide helpful feedback and guidance.

4. **Embrace constructive criticism**: Differentiate between destructive criticism and constructive feedback. While destructive criticism aims to tear you down, constructive feedback offers insights and suggestions for improvement. Be open to constructive criticism that can help refine your vision and strengthen it.

5. **Develop resilience**: Build emotional resilience to manage destructive criticism. Recognize that negative opinions or attacks on your vision often stem from the insecurities or biases of others and do not define your worth or the validity of your vision. Cultivate resilience by focusing on your goals, maintaining a positive mindset, and learning from setbacks.

6. **Reframe criticism as an opportunity**: Instead of viewing criticism as purely negative, reframe it as an opportunity for growth and learning. Assess the validity of the criticism,

extract any useful insights, and use it as a catalyst for self-improvement and refining your vision.

7. **Stay focused on your goals**: Maintain a clear focus on your goals and the vision you have for yourself. Avoid getting distracted or discouraged by destructive criticism. Keep your eyes on the prize and remain committed to pursuing your vision despite the negativity.

8. **Practice self-care**: Take care of yourself emotionally, mentally, and physically. Engage in activities that recharge and rejuvenate you. Surround yourself with positivity, engage in self-reflection, and practice self-compassion to counteract the effects of destructive criticism.

Have it at the back of your mind that it is your vision and your journey. By staying true to yourself, seeking support from the right people, and developing resilience, you can protect yourself from destructive criticism and continue to pursue your vision with determination and confidence.

NEHEMIAH: A CASE STUDY IN HANDLING OPPOSITION AGAINST VISION (NEHEMIAH 4)

The book of Nehemiah in the Bible tells the story of Nehemiah, a Jewish leader who was appointed by the Persian king to rebuild the walls of Jerusalem and restore the city after the Babylonians had destroyed it. In the story, Nehemiah faced many challenges, including opposition from neighboring nations and resistance from some of the people of Jerusalem.

However, despite these obstacles, Nehemiah was able to stay focused on his vision of rebuilding the city and was able to successfully complete the project.

One of the main themes in the book of Nehemiah is the importance of vision and perseverance. Nehemiah's vision of rebuilding the city was attacked by the neighboring nations and some of the people of Jerusalem.

They mocked him and tried to discourage him, but Nehemiah did not let their words or actions deter him from his mission. He was able to remain steadfast in his determination to see his vision come to fruition.

Nehemiah perfectly exemplifies the importance of having a clear vision, and the determination to see it through despite any obstacles or opposition that may come. His actions also highlight the importance of perseverance, and how it can help to overcome any obstacle and achieve success, regardless of any opposition.

Nehemiah's story in the Bible offers valuable insights for women facing opposition against their vision. And personally, in my endeavor as a purposeful and visionary woman, I have drawn vital lessons from Nehemiah's life.

Nehemiah 4:1-9

1 When Sanballat heard that we were rebuilding the wall he exploded in anger, vilifying the Jews.

2 In the company of his Samaritan cronies and military he let loose: "What are these miserable Jews doing? Do they think they can get everything back to normal overnight? Make building stones out of make-believe?"

3 At his side, Tobiah the Ammonite jumped in and said, "That is right! What do they think they are building? Why, if a fox climbed that wall, it would fall to pieces under his weight."

* * *

4 Nehemiah prayed, "Oh listen to us, dear God. We are so despised: Boomerang their ridicule on their heads; have their enemies cart them off as war trophies to a land of no return; do not forgive their iniquity, do not wipe away their sin—they've insulted the builders!"

[6] We kept at it, repairing and rebuilding the wall. The whole wall was soon joined together and halfway to its intended height because the people had a heart for the work.

[7] When Sanballat, Tobiah, the Arabs, the Ammonites, and the Ashdodites heard that the repairs of the walls of Jerusalem were going so well—that the breaks in the wall were being fixed—they were absolutely furious.

[8] They put their heads together and decided to fight against Jerusalem and create as much trouble as they could.

[9] We countered with prayer to our God and set a round-the-clock guard against them."

Nehemiah's assignment was the construction of the wall, which is comparable to the challenges many visionaries' encounter.

As a visionary, you may face opposition arising from others who perceive you as arrogant for undertaking what others have not done. This can evoke negative emotions such as envy, anger, and jealousy, even in those within your own circle.

It is important to recognize that the devil can use such individuals to test your courage and determination. If you succumb to fear and retreat, it indicates a lack of readiness for the assignment, and God may choose to replace you with someone else.

Let us examine Nehemiah's response when he encountered opposition from Sanballat, Tobiah, and Geshem:

1. **Firm Resolve**: Nehemiah displayed a firm resolve in the face of opposition. He remained steadfast and committed to his

vision, refusing to be deterred by the negativity or threats directed at him.

2. **Prayerful Dependence**: Nehemiah turned to God in prayer, seeking divine guidance, wisdom, and strength. He recognized the importance of relying on God's assistance to overcome the challenges he faced. You can emulate this by seeking spiritual guidance and drawing strength from his faith.

3. **Discernment and Wisdom**: Nehemiah exercised discernment and wisdom when he dealt with his opponents. He assessed their motives and actions, identifying their attempts to distract or intimidate him. You should develop the ability to discern the true intentions behind criticism or opposition, this would enable you to respond with wisdom and grace.

4. **Strategic Planning**: Nehemiah formulated strategic plans to counteract the opposition he encountered. He devised strategies to address specific challenges and mobilized resources accordingly. Similarly, you should engage in thoughtful planning, considering potential obstacles and developing practical strategies to overcome them.

5. **Unity and Collaboration**: Nehemiah fostered unity in his team and encouraged collaborative efforts. He motivated his co-laborers and reminded them of the significance of their collective purpose. You can build strong networks and cultivate a sense of unity, having others rally round your vision and gaining support in the face of opposition.

EIGHT VITAL STEPS YOU NEED TO TAKE IN PURSUING YOUR OWN VISION

1. **Clarity of Vision**: Nehemiah had a clear vision to rebuild the walls of Jerusalem. Similarly, you should have a well-defined and compelling vision for your goals. When you have a clear sense of purpose, it becomes easier for you to withstand opposition.

2. **Prayer and Reflection**: Nehemiah sought guidance from God through prayer and reflection before taking action. You can follow this example by seeking inner wisdom, guidance, and strength through prayer or meditation to help you navigate challenges.

3. **Preparation and Planning**: Nehemiah developed a detailed plan to accomplish his vision, considering potential obstacles and the resources required. You should invest time in strategic planning, understand the practical steps required to achieve your goals and anticipate potential opposition.

4. **Persistence and Determination:** Nehemiah faced various forms of opposition; ridicule and threats. Despite the challenges, he remained steadfast in pursuing his vision. Women can draw inspiration from Nehemiah's resilience, staying determined in the face of obstacles and refusing to give up on their goals.

5. **Surrounding Oneself with Supportive Allies**: Nehemiah enlisted the support of like-minded individuals who shared his vision. You as a woman should seek out a supportive network of allies who believe in your vision and can provide encouragement, advice, and practical assistance during challenging times.

6. **Responding with Wisdom and Discernment:** Nehemiah encountered attempts to distract and entrap him, but he responded with wisdom and discernment. You can learn from this example by carefully assessing criticism, considering the

intentions behind it, and responding in a manner that aligns with your vision and values.

7. **Focusing on the Greater Purpose:** Nehemiah consistently reminded himself and his followers of the greater purpose behind their vision. Women should stay focused on the positive impact their vision can make and use it as motivation to persevere despite opposition.

8. **Celebrating Progress and Milestones:** Nehemiah celebrated milestones along the way, acknowledging and appreciating the progress made. Women should take time to celebrate their achievements, both big and small, to maintain morale and reinforce their commitment to their vision.

The *Nehemiah Approach*, a tried-and-tested strategy that I have employed as a visionary, consistently delivers remarkable results. It effectively silences skeptics and instills tremendous strength and courage within me, fueling my pursuit of even more significant endeavors.

It is crucial to recognize that God entrusts the most important tasks to individuals who demonstrate bravery.

By studying Nehemiah's example, you can find inspiration, wisdom, and practical strategies to withstand opposition against your vision.

Applying these lessons can empower you to stay resilient, confident, and focused as you pursue your goals. These will help you overcome obstacles and stay committed to your assignments, bringing your visions to fruition.

PART SIX

THE POWER OF PASSION FOR A PURPOSEFUL WOMAN

Understanding Passion

Passion is a powerful and often underestimated force that plays a crucial role in keeping the flame of purpose and vision alive. When you have a deep passion for something, it fuels your motivation, determination, and perseverance. It is the driving force behind your unwavering commitment to pursuing your dreams and aspirations.

Passion adds a sense of purpose and meaning to your endeavors. It ignites a fire within you and propels you forward even in the face of challenges and setbacks. It gives you the energy and enthusiasm you need to overcome obstacles, push through barriers, and stay focused on your long-term vision.

Passion also breeds resilience. When you are passionate about what you do, you are more likely to bounce back from failures and setbacks. Enthusiastic individuals view challenges as opportunities for growth and learning rather than reasons to give up. They approach obstacles with determination, finding creative solutions and adopting strategies to surmount them.

Passion also has a ripple effect and inspires others. When you exude genuine passion for your purpose and vision, you become a source of inspiration for those around you. Your enthusiasm is contagious and can motivate others to pursue their own dreams. Passionate individuals have the ability to receive support, build strong teams, and foster a collective sense of purpose and dedication in them.

While skills, knowledge, and experience are important, passion is the driving force that propels you forward and gives your work a sense of purpose and fulfillment. It conveys joy, satisfaction, and fosters a deep sense of alignment with your true calling.

In summary, passion is not just a fleeting emotion; it is a fundamental element that sets your journey in motion toward purpose and vision. Embracing and nurturing your passion keeps you connected to your dreams, sustains your motivation, and empowers you to overcome challenges. So, never underestimate the power your passion exerts to drive your pursuit of purpose and keep the flame of your vision burning brightly.

As a woman, you can harness passion to fulfill your purpose and vision through these eight measures:

1. **Identify Your Passions**: Take the time to reflect on what truly ignites your enthusiasm and brings you joy. Identify your passions, whether they are related to career, hobbies, relationships, or personal growth. Understand what you are passionate about and you will have a strong foundation for building your purpose and vision and aligning them accordingly.

2. **Clarify Your Purpose:** Define your purpose by identifying what you deeply care about and what you feel called to contribute to the world. Your purpose should align with your passions and reflect your values and strengths. Clarifying your purpose helps you create a clear direction and focus for your actions.

3. **Set Visionary Goals**: Develop a compelling vision for your life and set goals that align with your purpose and passions. A visionary goal is inspiring, and it stretches you beyond your comfort zone. It should reflect your deepest desires and aspirations. Set specific, measurable, achievable, relevant, and time-bound (SMART) goals to turn your vision into reality.

4. **Cultivate Self-Belief:** Believe in yourself and your abilities. Recognize your unique strengths, talents, and experiences that can contribute to the fulfillment of your purpose and vision. Build confidence by learning from challenges and

celebrating your achievements. Surround yourself with positive influences and supportive networks that uplift and encourage you.

5. **Take Action with Intention**: Passion alone is not enough; it must be coupled with intentional action. Break down your goals into actionable steps and consistently work toward them. Be proactive in seeking opportunities that align with your passions and purpose. Embrace challenges as growth opportunities and persevere as you encounter obstacles.

6. **Embrace Continuous Learning**: Stay curious and committed to learning. Actively seek out knowledge, skills, and experiences that enhance your abilities and deepen your understanding of your passions and purpose. Invest in personal and professional development through courses, workshops, books, mentors, or coaching to continually expand your capabilities.

7. **Find Supportive Communities:** Surround yourself with like-minded individuals who share similar passions and values. Join communities, networks, or groups that provide support, encouragement, and collaboration. Engage in meaningful conversations, share experiences, and learn from others who are also on their own purpose-driven journeys.

8. **Embrace Self-Care**: Prioritize self-care to sustain your passion and energy. Take time to recharge, nurture your well-being, and maintain a healthy work-life balance. Self-care activities such as exercising, meditating, engaging in hobbies,

and spending time with loved ones can help prevent burnout and keep your passion alive.

By harnessing passion and aligning it with purpose and vision, you can tap into your inner drive, overcome obstacles, and make meaningful contributions. Embracing passion fuels personal fulfillment, enables you to create positive change, and paves the way for a purposeful and impactful life.

THE POWER OF FOCUS FOR VISIONARIES

Focus refers to the ability to direct one's attention, energy, and concentration toward a specific task, goal, or object. It involves maintaining a clear and undistracted mental state, allowing for heightened awareness and attentiveness to the present moment.

When you are focused, you are able to block out irrelevant or distracting stimuli and channel your resources toward a singular objective. Focus is essential for achieving productivity, learning continuously, developing personally, accomplishing goals, and achieving a deep level of engagement and understanding in any given activity.

However, focus is not always easy to maintain, especially in today's world where there are many distractions.

HOW TO APPLY THE POWER OF DISCIPLINE TO ACHIEVE FOCUS

You can apply discipline to enhance focus by adopting these seven strategies:

1. **Establish a Routine**: Create a structured daily routine that includes dedicated time for focused work or activities. Set specific time blocks for important tasks and commit to sticking to those time limits. Having a consistent schedule helps train the mind to focus during those designated periods.

2. **Eliminate Distractions**: Identify and minimize potential distractions in your environment. This could involve setting your phone to silent mode or putting it in another room, closing unnecessary tabs on your computer, or finding a quiet and secluded space where you can concentrate without interruptions.

3. **Practice Mindfulness**: Engage in mindfulness exercises or meditation to cultivate present-moment awareness. This practice can help quiet the mind, reduce mental clutter, and improve your ability to focus on the task at hand.

4. **Prioritize and Set Goals**: Determine your priorities and set clear goals for yourself. When you have a clear sense of what is most important, you can focus your attention and efforts on

those specific areas, reducing the tendency to get distracted by less important tasks.

5. **Break Tasks into Smaller Steps**: Large or complex tasks can be overwhelming and make it challenging to maintain focus. Break them down into smaller, manageable steps, and focus on completing one step at a time. When you adopt this approach, you experience a sense of accomplishment with each completed step, and it helps you maintain motivation and focus throughout the process.

6. **Take Regular Breaks**: While it may seem counterintuitive, taking regular breaks can actually improve focus and productivity. Schedule short breaks during longer periods of focused work to rest and recharge. Use this time to stretch, move around, or engage in a brief activity that helps you relax and reset before returning to the task with renewed focus.

7. **Practice Self-Care**: Take care of your overall well-being, as it directly impacts your ability to focus. Get enough sleep, eat nutritious meals, exercise regularly, and manage stress effectively. When you prioritize self-care, you boost your mental and physical energy, which supports improved focus and concentration.

Note that discipline is a skill that develops over time with consistent practice. Be patient with yourself as you cultivate discipline and focus and celebrate your progress along the way.

PART SEVEN

AVOIDING SELF-COMPARISON AS A PURPOSEFUL AND VISIONARY WOMAN

What is Self-Comparison?

Self-comparison means evaluating oneself in relation to others. It involves measuring one's own qualities, achievements, or circumstances against those of others as a means of assessing one's worth, success, or progress. Self-comparison can occur in various aspects of life, including personal, academic, professional, and social domains.

It can take two main forms: upward comparison and downward comparison. Upward comparison involves comparing oneself to individuals who are perceived as superior in certain aspects, such as achievements, abilities, or possessions. This type of comparison may lead to feelings of inadequacy, self-doubt, or decreased self-esteem.

On the other hand, downward comparison involves comparing oneself to individuals who are perceived as less successful or fortunate. This type of comparison may provide a temporary boost to one's self-esteem or a sense of relief but can also perpetuate a cycle of feeling superior or complacent.

Both forms of self-comparison can have negative effects on one's well-being and personal growth. Constantly comparing yourself to others can create unrealistic expectations, feelings of dissatisfaction, and hinder your ability to focus on personal progress and goals. It can also lead to jealousy, resentment, and strained relationships.

To nurture a healthier mindset, shift your focus from external comparisons to self-awareness, self-acceptance, and self-improvement.

Embrace a growth mindset, acknowledge your unique strengths and accomplishments, set personal goals, and celebrate personal milestones. All these can help you cultivate a positive self-image and promote a sense of fulfillment independent of others' achievements or circumstances.

Practicing self-compassion and gratitude can also be beneficial in reducing the negative impact of self-comparison and nurturing a more positive and contented outlook.

HOW A PURPOSEFUL AND VISIONARY WOMAN CAN AVOID SELF COMPARISON

Avoiding self-comparison can be challenging, but with conscious effort and self-awareness, as a purposeful and visionary woman, you can take steps to minimize its impact. Here are seven strategies to implement:

1. **Define Your Own Measures of Success**: Instead of relying on external benchmarks or societal expectations, define your own criteria for success based on your unique values, aspirations, and goals. Shift the focus from comparison to personal growth and progress. This emphasizes the fulfillment of your purpose and vision.

2. **Cultivate Self-Acceptance and Self-Compassion:** Embrace self-acceptance by recognizing and appreciating your own strengths, accomplishments, and journey. Practice self-compassion by showing kindness and understanding toward yourself, especially during times of perceived failure or setbacks. Treat yourself with the same compassion and support you would offer to a friend.

3. **Focus on Personal Growth and Development**: Direct your energy toward continuous learning, improvement, and personal development. Set goals that are aligned with your

purpose and vision, and measure your progress based on your own growth trajectory. Celebrate your achievements and milestones, no matter how small, and acknowledge the unique path you are on.

4. **Surround Yourself with Supportive Peers**: Seek out a supportive community of like-minded individuals who uplift and inspire you. Surround yourself with individuals who share similar values and ambitions to foster a sense of camaraderie and collaboration rather than competition. Build connections with people who encourage personal growth and celebrate each other's successes.

5. **Practice Gratitude and Appreciation**: Shift your focus from what you lack or what others have to expressing gratitude for your own blessings, strengths, and opportunities. Regularly practice gratitude by acknowledging and appreciating the positive aspects of your life and journey. This mindset can help counteract feelings of comparison and foster contentment and fulfillment.

6. **Limit Exposure to Comparison Triggers:** Be mindful of the environments, social media platforms, or situations that trigger feelings of self-comparison. Limit your exposure to such triggers and prioritize activities and relationships that contribute positively to your growth and well-being. Focus on what truly matters to you and invest your time and energy accordingly.

7. **Embrace Collaboration and Support Others:** Instead of viewing other women as competitors, adopt a mindset of

collaboration and support. Celebrate the successes of others and offer encouragement and assistance when possible. Recognize that there is room for everyone to thrive and that supporting others does not diminish your own journey.

Remember that everyone's path is unique, and comparison only hinders personal growth and fulfillment. By shifting your focus inward, practicing self-acceptance, and nurturing a supportive network, you can maintain a purposeful and visionary mindset while avoiding the pitfalls of self-comparison.

PART EIGHT

DEALING WITH UNHEALTHY COMPETITION AS A PURPOSEFUL AND VISIONARY WOMAN

What is Unhealthy Competition?

Unhealthy competition refers to a competitive mindset or behavior that is detrimental to individuals, relationships, or environments involved. It is characterized by negative or harmful attitudes, actions, and outcomes. Here are seven key features of unhealthy competition:

1. **Lack of Sportsmanship**: Unhealthy competition often involves a disregard for fairness, respect, and ethical conduct. It may include cheating, sabotage, or undermining others to gain an advantage.

2. **Obsession with Winning:** The focus is solely on winning at all costs, disregarding the value of participation, personal growth, and collaboration. Winning becomes the sole measure of success, overshadowing other important aspects of the activity or relationship.

3. **Comparison and Envy**: Unhealthy competition fosters a constant need to compare oneself to others, leading to envy, resentment, and a negative self-image. The desire to outperform or surpass others can be driven by a fear of inadequacy or a need for validation.

4. **Deterioration of Relationships**: Unhealthy competition can strain or damage relationships. Instead of supporting and uplifting one another, individuals engage in harmful rivalries. This undermines teamwork, cooperation, and mutual growth.

5. **Negative Emotional Impact**: Unhealthy competition often creates high levels of stress, anxiety, and pressure. Individuals may experience negative emotions such as jealousy, anger, frustration, or disappointment, leading to a decrease in overall well-being.

6. **Fixed Mindset**: Unhealthy competition can foster a fixed mindset, where individuals believe that their abilities and worth are fixed and limited. This mindset can inhibit personal growth, creativity, and resilience.

7. **Loss of Enjoyment and Passion**: When competition becomes unhealthy, the joy and passion associated with the activity may diminish. The focus on winning can overshadow the intrinsic rewards and enjoyment of the process itself.

It is important to recognize and address unhealthy competition to promote a more positive and constructive approach. Encouraging healthy competition involves promoting fair play, emphasizing personal growth, fostering collaboration, and valuing individual strengths and efforts.

By focusing on personal improvement, cooperation, and supportive relationships, competition can become a positive force for growth and achievement.

HOW TO AVOID UNHEALTHY COMPETITION AS A PURPOSEFUL AND VISIONARY WOMAN

A purposeful and visionary woman can avoid unhealthy competition by adopting the following strategies:

1. **Focus on Personal Growth**: Shift your focus from comparing yourself to others to focusing on your own personal growth

and development. Set goals that align with your purpose and vision, and measure your progress based on your own journey rather than external benchmarks. Emphasize self-improvement, continuous learning, and reaching your full potential.

2. **Embrace Collaboration and Cooperation**: Instead of viewing others as competitors, embrace a mindset of collaboration and cooperation. Seek opportunities to work together, support one another, and celebrate each other's successes. Recognize that collective progress and constructive collaboration can lead to greater achievements for everyone involved.

3. **Celebrate Uniqueness and Individuality**: Embrace your unique strengths, talents, and experiences. Understand that your value lies in your distinct perspective and contributions. Avoid comparing yourself to others; appreciate the qualities that make you special and focus on leveraging them to make a positive impact.

4. **Cultivate a Supportive Network**: Surround yourself with like-minded individuals who uplift and support you. Build relationships with people who share similar values, aspirations, and a growth mindset. Create a community of support and encouragement where competition is replaced with collaboration and mutual growth.

5. **Practice Self-Compassion**: Be kind and compassionate toward yourself. Acknowledge that everyone has their own journey and struggles. Treat yourself with the same kindness

and understanding you would offer to a friend. When faced with challenges or setbacks, practice self-compassion by reframing failures as opportunities for growth and learning.

6. **Focus on Purpose and Vision**: Keep your focus on your purpose and vision rather than comparing yourself to others. Remind yourself of the greater impact you are striving to make and the alignment of your unique path with your vision. When your focus is rooted in purpose, external competition bears lesser significance.

7. **Limit Exposure to Negative Influences**: Be mindful of the environments, social media, or situations that trigger unhealthy competition or comparison. Limit your exposure to negative influences that promote a scarcity mindset or create unnecessary pressure. Carefully curate your online and offline experiences to prioritize positivity, inspiration, and growth.

8. **Practice Gratitude**: Cultivate a sense of gratitude for your own journey, accomplishments, and blessings. Regularly reflect on the progress you have made, the lessons you have learned, and the opportunities you have been given. Gratitude helps shift the focus from comparison to appreciation, fostering contentment and a positive mindset.

By focusing on personal growth, embracing collaboration, celebrating uniqueness, and maintaining a purpose-driven mindset, a purposeful and visionary woman can navigate from unhealthy competition and cultivate a supportive and empowering approach to success.

FINAL NOTE

Dear Woman,

I want to congratulate you for buying and reading this book. It means you are indeed ready to unlock and unleash your potential!

I want you to understand that in the pursuit of purpose and vision, challenges may arise, but know that you are capable of overcoming them. Embrace setbacks as steppingstones and use them to propel yourself forward. Remember, even the most successful women face hurdles, but they rise above them with unwavering determination.

Believe in yourself, trust your instincts, and never underestimate your potential. You are destined for greatness, and this book is your guiding light to unlocking the doors of opportunity and empowerment.

As you embrace your purpose and vision, remember that this journey is not meant to be taken alone. Seek support from like-minded individuals, surround yourself with positive influences, and celebrate the progress you make along the way.

May this book ignite a fire within you, reminding you that your dreams are within reach. You have the power to transform your life and inspire others around you.

Embrace your uniqueness, embrace your calling, and embrace your potential.

The world awaits your brilliance and the impact you are destined to make. Go forth with confidence and let your light shine brightly!

With utmost belief in your capabilities,

Oluwatosin Olajumoke Arodudu
#OOA

REFERENCES

Oluwatosin Olajumoke Arodudu Identity. (Feb 9, 2020) *Self-discovery, Purpose and Leadership*

Oluwatosin Olajumoke Arodudu The Visionary Life. (Dec 12, 2021) *A guide to your journey and path*

Myles Munroe Releasing Your Potential Expanded Edition. (Feb 1, 2007) *Exposing the Hidden You*

ABOUT THE AUTHOR

Oluwatosin Olajumoke Arodudu is a multi-talented individual, renowned writer, publisher, identity coach, and a visionary. Her journey into the world of writing began in 2016 when she started her own blog. Through blogging, Oluwatosin discovered her unique voice, setting the stage for her writing career to unfold.

In 2017, she displayed her literary talent by penning three books: "Motherhood and The Society," "From the Perspective of the Child," and "Life on the Street of Readlooks." These works resonated with readers and revealed her ability to delve into thought-provoking topics.

Recognizing her knack for publishing and helping aspiring authors bring their stories to life, Oluwatosin embraced her calling as a Publisher and Identity Coach in 2018. Through her guidance, she has empowered numerous writers to fulfill their dreams of becoming published authors.

In 2020, Oluwatosin authored a powerful book titled "Identity: Self-discovery, Purpose, and Leadership." This transformative work has touched the lives of many, leading them on a profound journey of self-discovery and inspiring them to live purposefully. Building on this success, she released her second power book, "The Visionary Life," in 2021.

Oluwatosin has gone on to establish a thriving coaching practice centered around Identity, Visionary Living, and Leadership. Her website, oluwatosinarodudu.com, offers courses and resources that empower individuals to unlock their true potentials and live lives aligned with their visions.

Beyond her literary and coaching endeavors, Oluwatosin is happily married to Dr. Oludunsin Arodudu, a globally recognized doctoral sustainability researcher. During the day, she brings her talents to an international charitable organization, serving as an Executive Assistant and Financial Officer. She is a loving and devoted mother to two wonderful children.

Oluwatosin Olajumoke Arodudu is a testament to the power of passion, creativity, and determination. Through her writing, coaching, and leadership, she continues to inspire others to embrace their true selves and embark on a visionary path of growth and fulfillment.

You can connect with her via this media:

- Website: oluwatosinarodudu.com

- Facebook: Oluwatosin Olajumoke Arodudu and Today's Woman Discovery

- Instagram: tw_discovery

- Email: ooainspires@gmail.com

- todayswomandiscovery@gmail.com

- oluwatosin@hadarcreations.com

OTHER BOOKS BY AUTHOR

THE DISCIPLINED WRITER

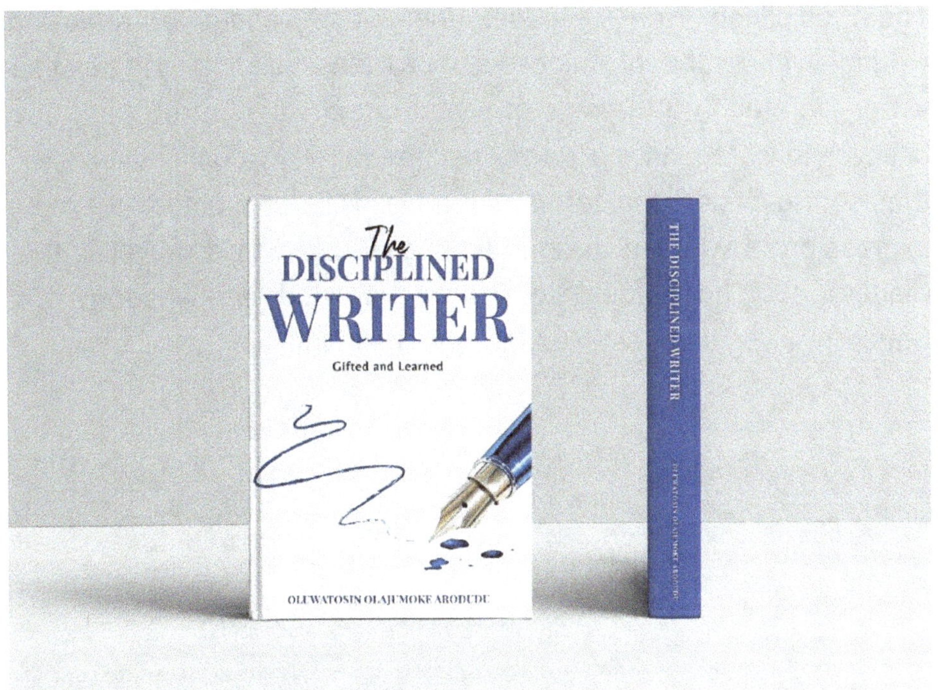

The Disciplined Writer is a guide to navigate the writing landscape with integrity. Through this invaluable book, writers will discover the significance of studying to show themselves approved and learn how to navigate the media as an influential force while staying true to their authentic voice.

The book unravels the gimmicks and challenges present in the media and writing world, offering practical advice on employing discipline and wisdom for self-preservation. By emphasizing the importance of knowledge and its proper application, Oluwatosin inspires writers via this book to go beyond mere talent and become well-informed individuals who can effectively impact people via their chosen writing niche.

The Disciplined Writer exposes the consequences of releasing writings without thoughtfulness and provides insight on the need for writers to stand on the side of wisdom and self-control. As a firm believer in safeguarding one's inspiration, Oluwatosin discovered that controversies can tarnish creative wells and hinder the pure expression of wisdom through writing. Oluwatosin's prayer is that readers of "The Disciplined Writer" will embrace wisdom and transform lives and destinies through their writing.

TRAPPED IN TRAUMA

A Workbook for Women on Unravelling Hidden Wounds and Thriving Beyond Trauma

"Trapped in Trauma: A Workbook for Women on Unraveling Hidden Wounds and Thriving Beyond Trauma" is a comprehensive and empowering guidebook designed to support women in their journey of healing from past traumas. With a compassionate approach and practical exercises, this workbook offers a transformative roadmap for untangling the complex layers of trauma and reclaiming a life of resilience, empowerment, and joy.

Written specifically for women who have experienced trauma, this workbook serves as a trusted companion on their path to healing. Drawing upon research, psychological insights, and the author's own experiences, each chapter addresses a crucial aspect of trauma recovery, guiding readers through a step-by-step process of self-discovery and healing.

In addition to providing tools for personal healing, "Trapped in Trauma" emphasizes the importance of self-care, self-compassion, and building a support network. The workbook highlights the significance of creating a safe space for oneself and seeking professional help when necessary, ensuring that readers have the resources and guidance they need along their healing journey.

Also, this workbook provides a nurturing environment for women to navigate their emotions, rewrite their narratives, and embrace their resilience as they work towards a future filled with hope and possibility.

This book is a valuable resource for any woman seeking to break free from the grip of trauma and embark on a path of self-discovery, healing, and transformation. By combining practical exercises, supportive guidance, and a compassionate approach, this workbook empowers women to unravel their hidden wounds and unlock their true potential for a life of thriving beyond trauma.

UNVEILED

Empowering Women on the Path of Self-Discovery invites you on a transformative journey of self-exploration and empowerment. It is specifically designed for women who are ready to embark on a path of self-discovery, unleashing their hidden potential and embracing their authentic selves.

Within the pages of this insightful book, you will embark on a profound journey of self-reflection and empowering discoveries. You will uncover your unique strengths, values, and purpose, leading you to a profound understanding of your true self.

As you progress through the book, you will gain valuable insights and clarity on various aspects of your life, including personal growth, relationships, career, and overall well-being. You will learn powerful techniques to overcome self-limiting beliefs, embrace self-compassion, and cultivate a positive mindset.

Unveiled serves as your trusted companion, providing a safe space for self-expression and self-exploration. It encourages you to embrace vulnerability, heal past wounds, and release self-imposed limitations. Each part of the book invites you to dive deeper into different aspects of your life, empowering you to create positive shifts, set meaningful goals, and live a life aligned with your true essence.

Whether you are seeking personal growth, embarking on a new chapter in life, or simply desiring a deeper understanding of yourself, "Unveiled" is your trusted companion on this profound journey. It empowers you to embrace your uniqueness, celebrate your strengths, and unlock the boundless potential within.

NURTURING EXCELLENCE

Building a Transformative Mentor-Mentee Relationship for Women" is an empowering and transformative guide that explores the unique dynamics of mentorship tailored specifically for women. This compelling book delves into the profound impact of mentorship in fostering excellence, growth, and empowerment. Through inspiring experiences and insightful wisdom, this book unravels the essence of a successful mentor-mentee relationship.

It emphasizes the importance of creating a supportive and empowering environment where women can thrive and reach their full potential. Drawing from real-life experiences, the book offers practical advice and actionable strategies for both mentors and mentees. Mentors discover how to provide guidance, share expertise, and empower their mentees to tap into their unique strengths and talents.

Mentees, on the other hand, learn to embrace opportunities for growth, seek mentorship, and navigate their journey with confidence. The book emphasizes the power of vulnerability, trust, and open communication, nurturing a bond that fosters growth and mutual respect. Readers are encouraged to set goals, collaborate, and celebrate the achievements of the mentor-mentee partnership.

As the mentor-mentee relationship blossoms, both parties experience personal and professional transformation. The book highlights the positive influence of mentorship in building resilience, self-belief, and a sense of purpose. "Nurturing Excellence" goes beyond individual growth, exploring how transformative mentorship can impact organizations, industries, and society as a whole. Whether a seasoned mentor or a mentee seeking guidance, "Nurturing Excellence" offers valuable insights and practical tools to foster a transformative mentor-mentee relationship that empowers and elevates women towards a future of excellence and fulfillment. This book serves as a powerful resource for women seeking to make a lasting impact in their personal and professional lives through the power of mentorship.

EMPOWERED LEADERSHIP

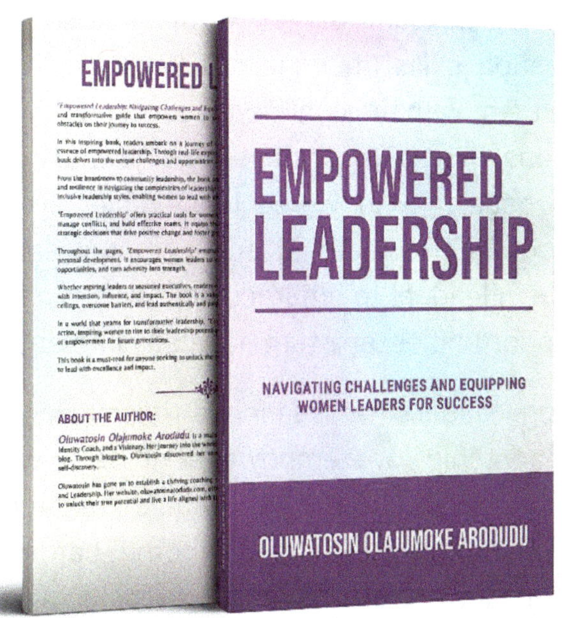

Navigating Challenges and Equipping Women Leaders for Success is a compelling and transformative guide that empowers women to embrace their leadership potential and overcome obstacles on their journey to success. In this inspiring book, readers embark on a journey of self-discovery and personal growth, exploring the essence of empowered leadership.

Through real-life experiences, expert insights, and practical strategies, the book delves into the unique challenges and opportunities that women leaders face in various spheres of life. From the boardroom to community leadership, the book addresses the importance of authenticity, self-belief, and resilience in navigating the complexities of leadership roles. It emphasizes the power of empowering and inclusive leadership styles, enabling women to lead with empathy, compassion, and vision. "Empowered Leadership" offers practical tools for women leaders to strengthen their communication skills, manage conflicts, and build effective teams. It equips them with the confidence and competence to make strategic decisions that drive positive change and foster growth. Throughout the pages, "Empowered Leadership" emphasizes the importance of continuous learning and personal development. It encourages women leaders to embrace a growth mindset, embrace challenges as opportunities, and turn adversity into strength.

Whether aspiring leaders or seasoned executives, readers of "Empowered Leadership" are empowered to lead with intention, influence, and impact. The book is a valuable resource for women seeking to shatter glass ceilings, overcome barriers, and lead authentically and purposefully in their professional and personal lives.

In a world that yearns for transformative leadership, "Empowered Leadership" serves as a powerful call to action, inspiring women to rise to their leadership potential, create positive change, and leave a lasting legacy of empowerment for future generations. This book is a must-read for anyone seeking to unlock the true potential of women leaders and empower them to lead with excellence and impact.

THE VISIONARY LIFE

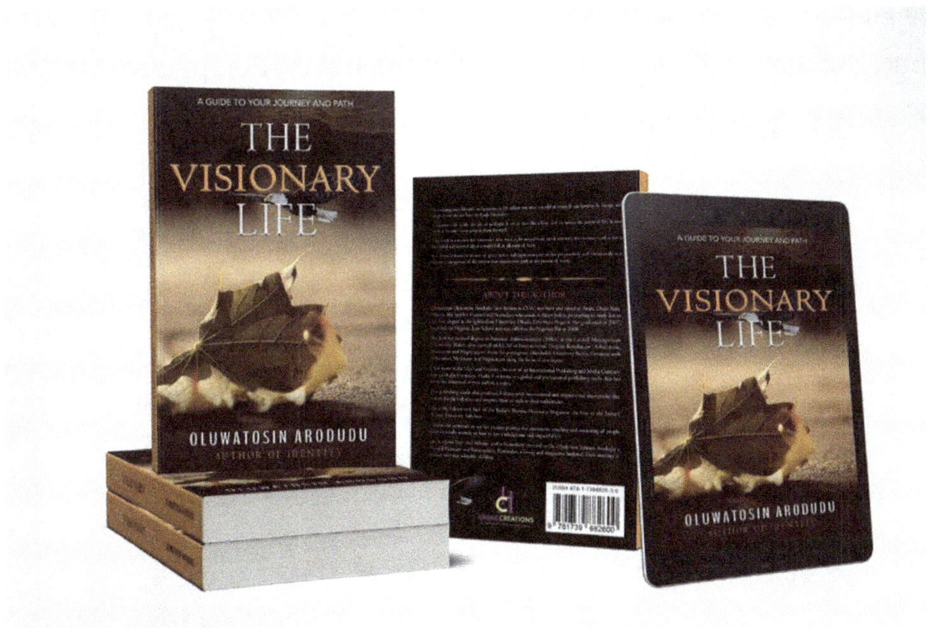

Discovering your Identity and purpose in life ushers you into a world of vision.

It can however be bumpy and rough if you do not have the eagle mentality.

A Visionary life is like the life of an eagle. It set its face like a flint, and no matter the storm of life, it rises above it because vision propels it forward.

This book is a manual for visionaries who want to be armed from inside out with the necessary tool to live a successful and focused life in a world full of all sorts of vices.

It is inspired from the throne of grace, and it will light your path to live purposefully and intentionally as a visionary irrespective of the storms that cross your path in the pursuit of vision.

IDENTITY

Many great minds are trapped and locked up in a cage as a result of their backgrounds and social conditioning. They are befuddled and shielded away from realizing their immense potential by defeatist mindsets and mental strangleholds in their subconscious. No matter what they hear, or who is around them to help them grow, they suffer from MIND BLOCKAGE and just cannot break out from their current mind hole.

IDENTITY is a reference book on personal development that identifies with, and describes the travails of the confused mind, while offering life coaching on transition to self-development and actualization. Identity tells the story of Oluwatosin's travails with mind entrapment and takes you through her journey to self-discovery, purpose, and leadership. The author's experience teaches valid lessons on breaking free from a perpetual state of mental helplessness and living a purposeful life. If deep down, you know you are made for more but are clueless about forging a path towards it, then this book is definitely for you. It is a book for aspiring leaders and leaders going through turmoil as a result of their strong personality. It coaches leaders with strong personalities on how to master, manage and weaponize their emotions to their own advantage, both as individuals and leaders in their sphere of influence.

All books by the author can be purchased via Amazon and www.hadarcreations.com.

Journal

Journal

www.ingramcontent.com/pod-product-compliance
Lightning Source LLC
Chambersburg PA
CBHW052055150726
48002CB00002B/902